COMMON LAW GRAND JURY HANDBOOK

JOHN DARASH

THE COMMON LAW GRAND JURY HANDBOOK
COPYRIGHT © 2020 BY JOHN DARASH
www.NationalLibertyAlliance.org
3979 Albany Post Road
Hyde Park, NY. 12538

COVER DESIGN: – John Darash

SPEAK TO THE AUTHOR – Mon. 9 PM – 11 PM EST
www.NationalLibertyAlliance.org/mondaycall

OTHER BOOKS BY JOHN DARASH
- Government by Consent Book
- Court Access and the Common Law
- Common Law Grand Jury Handbook
- Common Law Petit Jury Handbook
- Common Law Grand and Petit Jurist Handbook
- Committee of Safety Committeeman Handbook
- Committee of Safety Organizing Handbook
- Elected Official Common Law Handbook
- Sheriff's Common Law Handbook
- Elected Official's Handbook
- Jury Administrative Handbook
- Founding Documents Handbook
- Militia Handbook
- Roberts Rules of Order Handbook
- Memorandums of Common Law Handbook

All rights reserved. Printed in the United States of America; No part of this book may be reproduced or transmitted, downloaded, distributed, reversed engineered, or stored in or introduced into any information storage and retrieval system, in any form or by any means including photocopying and recording, whether electronic or mechanical, now known or hereinafter invented without permission in writing from the author.

ISBN: 9798673818732
(1) Common Law (2) American History (3) Ethics (4) Science of Natural Law

PURPOSE OF THIS HANDBOOK:

This Handbook will acquaint persons who have been selected to serve on a common law Grand Jury with the general nature and importance of their role as grand jurors. It explains some of the terms that grand jurors will encounter during their service and offers some suggestions helpful to them in performing this important public service. It is intended that this Handbook will, to a degree, provide a permanent record of much of the information presented in the Grand Jury orientation. Grand jurors are encouraged to refer to this Handbook periodically throughout their service to reacquaint themselves with their duties and responsibilities.

There is a war that has been raging since antiquity. It is a war for our hearts and our minds, for our flesh, for our very souls; to bring all mankind under a one world order (novus ordo seclorum). As George Washington put it in his Fair Well Address "...*orchestrated by a small group of cunning, ambitious, and unprincipled men who have subverted the power of the People and usurped for themselves the reins of government. They have put in the place of the delegated will of the nation the will of a small but artful and enterprising minority to make the public administration the mirror of their ill-concerted and incongruous projects of faction, rather than the organ of consistent and wholesome plans digested by common counsels and modified by mutual interests.*"

Because government 'FAILED' in their duty to assure a proper education in our schools, it is the duty of the People to self-educate, educate their sheriff, and educate our children. This is the purpose of these Series of Handbooks, and the books Government by Consent and Court Access and the Common law.

Today Liberty and our very way of life are under attack. Because We the People are ignorant of the true Law of the Land and our History, we have lost our way! It's not until we start to read about what we have inherited from our founding fathers that we start to realize how far we have drifted from the blessings of Liberty. But, there is hope.

Thomas Jefferson said, *"The purpose of government is to enable the People of a nation to live in safety and happiness. Government exists for the interests of the governed, not for the governors. The tax which will be paid for the purpose of education is not more than the thousandth part of what will be paid to kings, priests and nobles who will rise up among us if we leave the People in ignorance. Educate and inform the whole mass of the People... They are the only sure reliance for the preservation of our liberty. I know no safe depositary of the ultimate powers of the society but the People themselves; and if we think them not enlightened enough to exercise their control with a wholesome discretion, the remedy is not to take it from them, but to inform their discretion by education. This is the true corrective of abuses of constitutional power. An enlightened citizenry is indispensable for the proper functioning of a republic. Self-government is not possible unless the citizens are educated sufficiently to enable them to exercise oversight. It is therefore imperative that the nation see to it that a suitable education be provided for all its citizens."*

TABLE OF CONTENTS

Purpose of this Handbook	3
Table of Contents	5
Introduction	7
Grand Jury	11
A Fixture in its Own Right	14
Law notes Magna Carta #52	15
Law notes Magna Carta #61	16
Can Investigate Merely on Suspicion	18
The Fox & the Hen House	19
Kentucky Resolutions	20
Grand Jury Origin and History	20
Common Law	22
Courts without Honor	24
Maxims on Principals of Common Law	25
Maxims on Legitimacy of Gov	26
Maxims on Testimony and Evidence	26
Maxims on Civic Duty of Citizens	27
Maxims on Private Property	27
Maxims on Unalienable Rights	27
Maxims on Crime and Punishment	28
Maxims on Judicial Reasoning	28
Nature of the Grand Jury	29
The Grand Jury's Tasks	31
Investigation	31
Selection of Jurors	32
Organization, Oath, and Officers	32
Procedure	33
Secrecy	37
Protection of Grand Jurors	38
Practical Suggestions for Grand Jurors	39
Jurist VOW	40
Glossary of Terms	42
Bill of Rights	44
Declaration of Independence	46
US Constitution	54
Founding Fathers to this generation	73

NOTICE: *The content of this book are not the interpretation or the opinion of the author. But is documented history of the words of our Founders and decisions in Courts of Justice by the States and United States Supreme Courts.*

INTRODUCTION

GOVERNMENT BY CONSENT: "Under our system of government upon the individuality and intelligence of the citizen, the state does not claim to control him, except as his conduct to others, leaving him the sole judge as to all that affects himself."[1] "Every man is independent of all laws, except those prescribed by nature, a/k/a Common Law, and "is not bound by any institutions formed by his fellowman without his consent."[2] "The sovereignty of a state does not reside in the persons who fill the different departments of its government, but in the People, from whom the government emanated; and they may change it at their discretion. Sovereignty, then in this country, abides with the constituency, and not with the agent; and this remark is true, both in reference to the federal and state government."[3]

"In the United States, sovereignty resides in people. Congress cannot invoke the sovereign power of the People to override their will."[4] Therefore, "sovereignty itself is, of course, not subject to law, for it is the author and source of law; but in our system, while sovereign powers are delegated to the agencies of government, sovereignty itself remains with the people, by whom and for whom all government exists and acts And the Common Law, Declaration of Independence, US Constitution, and the Bill of Rights are the definition and limitation of power." In the preamble to our United States Constitution, "*We the People*" said:

---

[1] Mugler v. Kansas 123 U.S. 623, 659-60.
[2] Cruden v. Neale, 2 N.C. 338 (1796) 2 S.E.
[3] Spooner v. McConnell, 22 F 939 @ 943.
[4] Perry v. US, 294 U.S330.

"We the people of the United States, in order to form a more perfect union, establish justice, insure domestic tranquility, provide for the common defense, promote the general welfare, and secure the blessings of liberty to ourselves and our posterity, do ordain and establish this Constitution for the United States of America."

Thereby, "ordaining" the Constitution as the Law of the Land declared in Article VI, clause 2 where *"We the People"* said: *"This Constitution, and the Laws of the United States which shall be made in pursuance thereof; and all treaties made, or which shall be made, under the Authority of the United States, shall be the Supreme Law of the Land; and the Judges in every State shall be bound thereby; anything in the Constitution or Laws of any State to the Contrary notwithstanding."*

In Article III Section 2 clause 1, *"We the People"* said, *"The judicial power shall extend to all cases, in law and equity, arising under this Constitution, the laws of the United States."* In Article I Section 1 We the Sovereign People herein, *"vested all legislative powers in Congress,"* and we defined that legislative power in Article I section 8.

Whereas, Congress wrote fifty-seven (57) US Codes that govern 'courts of equity.' These codes are codes, statutes and regulations that govern government agencies and commercial activities. For example, USC Title 2 governs Congress, USC Title 3 governs President, USC Title 6 governs Homeland Security, USC Title 7 governs Agriculture, USC Title 10 governs Armed Forces, USC Title 12 governs Banks and Banking, USC Title 14 governs Coast Guard, USC Title 34 governs Navy, USC Title 39 governs Postal

Service, etc. Therefore, "all codes, rules, and regulations are for government authorities only, not human creators in accordance with God's laws."[5]

We the People wrote the Common Law Declaration of Independence, the foundation of all American Law where we covenanted with God declaring: "We hold these truths to be self-evident, that all men are created equal, that they are endowed by their Creator with certain unalienable Rights, that among these are Life, Liberty and the pursuit of Happiness.--That to secure these rights, Governments are instituted among Men, deriving their just powers from the consent of the governed."

Thereby, We the Sovereign People created a Republic and ordained in Article IV Section 4 that: "The United States shall guarantee to every state in this union a Republican form of government, and shall protect each of them against invasion; and on application of the legislature, or of the executive (when the legislature cannot be convened) against domestic violence."

"A Republican government is one in which the powers of sovereignty are vested in the people and are exercised by the people, either directly, or through representatives chosen by the people, to whom those powers are specially delegated."[6] "For, the very idea that man may be compelled to hold his life, or the means of living, or any material right essential to the enjoyment of life, at the mere will of another, seems to be intolerable

---

[5] Rodriques v. Ray Donavan (U.S. Department of Labor) 769 F. 2d 1344, 1348 (1985).

[6] In re Duncan, 139 U.S. 449, 11 S.Ct. 573, 35 L.Ed. 219; Minor v. Happersett, 88 U.S. (21 Wall.) 162, 22 L.Ed. 627." Black's Law Dictionary, Fifth Edition, p. 626.

in any country where freedom prevails, as being the essence of slavery itself."[7]

The United States is the second "Lawful Republic" in history. The first, being Israel about 1400 BC. This is why our founding fathers referred to America as "New Israel." For, like Israel We the People in 1789, placed ourselves under the same Law that Israel lived under, a/k/a "Common Law" or "Natural Law:" And it is in these "Courts of Law" alone where People are judged by a jury of their peers, the People and not the government whereas; "His majesty [natures God] in the eye of the law is always present in all his courts, though he cannot personally distribute justice.[8] His judges [Grand jury] are the mirror by which the King's image [Justice] is reflected."[9]

A lawful Republic receives its powers from 'Natures God' who through our covenant [Declaration of Independence] with Him, in a desire to be ruled by God and not man, blessed us with liberty and the unalienable right to have government by consent whereas, we wrote the Constitution and its capstone Bill of Rights to bind down government. And one of the ways we consent or not to government is in the courts via the Grand and Petit Jury. Two other ways are through Committees of Safety and the militia. Learn more - www.NationalLibertyAlliance.org.

---

[7] Yick Wo v. Hopkins, 118 US 356, 370 Quotiens dubia interpretatio libertatis est, secundum libertatem respondendum erit.
[8] Fortesc.c.8. 2Inst.186.
[9] 1 Blackstone's Commentaries, 270, Chapter 7, Section 379.

GRAND JURY

"The Jury is the Achilles heel of tyrants."
– HG Wells

The Grand Jury is one of the ways that We the People Consent to the actions of our government.[10] "If anyone has been deprived of their unalienable right, we will immediately grant full justice therein." The will of the Grand Jury is the opening and manifestation of due process[11] in a court of law. The Grand Jury is the "Sureties of the Peace" that we find in the Magna Carta that was ordained by the People through the 5th Amendment[12] and, thereby officially acknowledged as an unalienable right. They are the posterity of our founding fathers. They are *"We the People"* that ordained and established the Constitution for the officers of this court to proceed with authority.

Justice Powell, in United States v. Calandra[13] stated, "The institution of the grand jury is deeply rooted in Anglo-American history; [n3] In England, the grand jury [p343] served for centuries, both as a body of accusers, sworn to

---

[10] **Declaration of Independence:** We hold these truths to be self-evident, that all men are created equal, that they are endowed by their Creator with certain unalienable Rights, that among these are Life, Liberty and the pursuit of Happiness. That to secure these rights, Governments are instituted among Men, deriving their just powers from the consent of the governed.

[11] "**Due course of law**, this phrase is synonymous with "due process of law" or "law of the land" and means law in its regular course of administration through courts of justice." - Kansas Pac. Ry. Co. v. Dunmeyer 19 KAN 542.

[12] **Amendment V:** No person shall be held to answer for a capital, or otherwise infamous crime, unless on a presentment or indictment of a Grand Jury ... nor be deprived of life, liberty, or property, without due process of law.

[13] 414 U.S. 338, 343 (1974)

discover, and present for trial, persons suspected of criminal wrongdoing; and, as a protector of citizens against arbitrary and oppressive governmental action. In this country, the Founders thought the grand jury so essential to basic liberties, that they provided, in the Fifth Amendment, that federal prosecution for serious crimes can only be instituted by a 'presentment or indictment of a Grand Jury.'" Cf. Costello v. United States, 350 U.S. 359, 361-362 (1956). "The grand jury's historic functions survive to this day. Its responsibilities determination whether there is probable cause to believe a crime has been committed, and the protection of citizens against unfounded criminal prosecutions." Branzburg v. Hayes, 408 U.S. 665, 686-687 (1972)."

"If any of our civil servants shall have transgressed against any of the people in any respect; and, they shall ask us (Common Law Grand Jury) *to cause that error to be amended without delay; or, shall have broken some one of the articles of peace or security; and, their transgression shall have been shown to four Jurors of the twenty five; and, if those four Jurors are unable to settle the transgression, they shall come to the twenty-five, showing to the Grand Jury the error which shall be enforced by the law of the land."* - Magna Carta, June 15, A.D. 1215, 61 (First recorded Grand Jury)

The People have the unbridled right to empanel and preside over their own proceedings unfettered by technical rules and to investigate merely on suspicion. It is the Grand Jury's function to consider criminal charges whereas prosecutors have no authority to change or negotiate away the Grand Jury's indictments. Indictments are final and any additional charges cannot be added without the consent of the grand jury.

"The constitutions of most of our states assert that all power is inherent in the people; that they may exercise it by themselves, in all cases to which they think themselves competent, as in electing their functionaries executive and legislative, and deciding by a jury of themselves, both fact and law, in all judiciary cases in which any fact is involved ..."[14]

In the U.S. Supreme Court case of United States v. Williams,[15] Justice Antonin Scalia, writing for the majority, confirmed that; *"The American grand jury is neither part of the judicial, executive nor legislative branches of government, but instead belongs to the people. It is in effect a fourth branch of government 'governed' and administered to directly by and on behalf of the American people, and its authority emanates from the Bill of Rights. Thus,* [People] *have the unbridled right to empanel their own grand juries and present 'True Bills' of indictment to a court, which is then required to commence a criminal proceeding."* Our Founding Fathers presciently thereby created a 'buffer' the people may rely upon for 'justice,' when public officials, including judges, criminally violate the law.

Natural Law demands that only the People via 'free and independent Grand Juries have the Supreme Judicial Authority to indict or not, to decide the law, to sit as the tribunal in all criminal cases that come before it, to nullify any statute, to deny any rules, to indict or not, Tribunals are established in 25 unalienable sovereigns whose

---

[14] Thomas Jefferson, letter to John Cartwright; June 5, 1824.
[15] 112 S.Ct. 1735, 504 U.S. 36, 118 L.Ed.2d 352 (1992).

decisions are final and cannot be ignored or altered.

"*Although the grand jury normally operates, of course, in the courthouse and under judicial auspices, its institutional relationship with the judicial branch has traditionally been, so to speak, at arm's length.*" – United States v. Calandra, 414 U.S. 338, 343, 94 S.Ct. 613, 617, 38 L.Ed.2d 561 (1974); Fed. Rule Crim. Proc. 6(a).

GRAND JURY IS A CONSTITUTIONAL FIXTURE IN ITS OWN RIGHT:[16]

In United States v. Calandra, quoted in US v Williams, the United States Supreme Court said: "*The grand jury is an institution separate from the courts, over whose functioning the courts do not preside. The "common law" of the Fifth Amendment demands the traditional functioning of the grand jury. The grand jury is an institution separate from the courts, over whose functioning the courts do not preside, we think it clear that, as a general matter at least, no such "supervisory" judicial authority exists. "[R]ooted in long centuries of Anglo-American history,"*[17] *the grand jury is mentioned in the Bill of Rights, but not in the body of the Constitution. It has not been textually assigned, therefore, to any of the branches described in the first three Articles. It*" '*is a constitutional fixture in its own right.*'"[18] In

---

[16] United States v. Williams, 112 S.Ct. 1735, 504 U.S. 36, 118 L.Ed.2d 352 (1992).
[17] Hannah v. Larche, 363 U.S. 420, 490, 80 S.Ct. 1502, 1544, 4 L.Ed.2d 1307 (1960) (Frankfurter, J., concurring in result).
[18] United States v. Chanen, 549 F.2d 1306, 1312 (CA9 1977) (quoting Nixon v. Sirica, 159 U.S.App.D.C. 58, 70, n. 54, 487 F.2d 700, 712, n. 54 (1973)), cert. denied, 434 U.S. 825, 98 S.Ct. 72, 54 L.Ed.2d 83 (1977).

fact the whole theory of its function is that it belongs to no branch of the institutional government, serving as a kind of buffer or referee between the Government and the people.[19] *Although the grand jury normally operates, of course, in the courthouse and under judicial auspices, its institutional relationship with the judicial branch has traditionally been, so to speak, at arm's length. Judges' direct involvement in the functioning of the grand jury has generally been confined to the constitutive one of calling the grand jurors together and administering their oaths of office"*[20]

LAW NOTES MAGNA CARTA #52.

If anyone shall have been disseized by us, or removed, without a legal sentence of his peers, from his lands, castles, liberties or lawful right, we shall straightway restore them to him. And if a dispute shall arise concerning this matter it shall be settled according to the judgment of the twenty-five barons who are mentioned below as sureties for the peace. But with regard to all those things of which any one was, by king Henry our father or king Richard our brother, disseized or dispossessed without legal judgment of his peers, which we have in our hand or which others hold, and for which we ought to give a guarantee: We shall have respite until the common term for crusaders. Except with regard to those concerning

---

[19] Stirone v. United States, 361 U.S. 212, 218, 80 S.Ct. 270, 273, 4 L.Ed.2d 252 (1960); Hale v. Henkel, 201 U.S. 43, 61, 26 S.Ct. 370, 373, 50 L.Ed. 652 (1906); G. Edwards, The Grand Jury 28-32 (1906).
[20] United States v. Calandra, 414 U.S. 338, 343, 94 S.Ct. 613, 617, 38 L.Ed.2d 561 (1974); Fed.Rule Crim.Proc. 6(a).

which a plea was moved, or an inquest made by our order, before we took the cross. But when we return from our pilgrimage, or if, by chance, we desist from our pilgrimage, we shall straightway then show full justice regarding them.

LAW NOTES MAGNA CARTA #61.

Inasmuch as for the sake of God, and for the bettering of our realm, and for the more ready healing of the discord which has arisen between us and our barons, we have made all these aforesaid concessions,--wishing them to enjoy forever entire and firm stability, we make and grant to them the following security: That the barons (*Free Men*), namely, may elect at their pleasure twenty five barons from the realm, who ought, with all their strength, to observe, maintain and cause to be observed, the peace and privileges which we have granted to them and confirmed by this our present charter. In such wise, namely, that if we, our justice, or our bailiffs, or any one of our servants shall have transgressed against any one in any respect, or shall have broken some one of the articles of peace or security, and our transgression shall have been shown to four barons of the aforesaid twenty five: those four barons shall come to us, or, if we are abroad, to our justice, showing to us our error; and they shall ask us to cause that error to be amended without delay.

And if we do not amend that error, or, we being abroad, if our justice do not amend it within a term of forty days from the time when it was shown to us or, we being abroad, to our justice: the aforesaid four barons shall refer the matter to the remainder of the twenty five barons, and those twenty five barons, with the whole land in common, shall distrain and oppress us in every way in their power,--namely, by taking our castles, lands and possessions, and in every other way that they can, until amends shall have been made according to their judgment. Saving the persons of ourselves, our queen, and our children.

And when amends shall have been made they shall be in accord with us as they had been previously. And whoever of the land wishes to do so, shall swear that in carrying out all the aforesaid measures he will obey the mandates of the aforesaid twenty five barons, and that, with them, he will oppress us to the extent of his power. And, to anyone who wishes to do so, we publicly and freely give permission to swear; and we will never prevent anyone from swearing.

Moreover, all those in the land who shall be unwilling, themselves and of their own accord, to swear to the twenty five barons as to distraining and oppressing us with them: such ones we shall make to swear by our mandate, as has been said. And if any one of the twenty five barons shall die, or leave the country, or in any other way be prevented from carrying out the aforesaid measures,--the remainder of the aforesaid twenty five barons shall choose another in his place, according to their judgment, who shall be sworn in the same way as the others.

Moreover, in all things entrusted to those twenty five barons to be carried out, if those twenty five shall be present and chance to disagree among themselves with regard to some matter, or if some of them, having been summoned, shall be unwilling or unable to be present: that which the majority of those present shall decide or decree shall be considered binding and valid, just as if all the twenty five had consented to it. And the aforesaid twenty five shall swear that they will faithfully observe all the foregoing, and will cause them to be observed to the extent of their power. And we shall obtain nothing from any one, either through ourselves or through another, by which any of those concessions and liberties may be revoked or diminished. And if any such thing shall have been obtained, it shall be vain and invalid, and we shall never make use of it either through ourselves or through another.

GRAND JURY CAN INVESTIGATE MERELY ON SUSPICION:[21]

The United States Supreme Court in US v Williams went on to say: "The grand jury's functional independence from the judicial branch is evident both in the scope of its power to investigate criminal wrongdoing, and in the manner in which that power is exercised. Unlike [a] [c]ourt, whose jurisdiction is predicated upon a specific case or controversy, the grand jury 'can investigate merely on suspicion that the law is being violated, or even because it wants assurance that it is not.'"[22] It need not identify the offender it suspects, or even "the precise nature of the offense" it is investigating.[23] The grand jury requires no authorization from its constituting court to initiate an investigation,[24] nor does the prosecutor require leave of court to seek a grand

---

[21] United States v. Williams, 112 S.Ct. 1735, 504 U.S. 36, 118 L.Ed.2d 352 (1992).
[22] United States v. R. Enterprises, 498 U.S. ----, ---- , 111 S.Ct. 722, 726, 112 L.Ed.2d 795 (1991) (quoting United States v. Morton Salt Co., 338 U.S. 632, 642-643, 70 S.Ct. 357, 364, 94 L.Ed. 401 (1950)).
[23] Blair v. United States, 250 U.S. 273, 282, 39 S.Ct. 468, 471, 63 L.Ed. 979 (1919).
[24] see Hale, supra, 201 U.S., at 59-60, 65, 26 S.Ct., at 373, 375.

jury indictment. And in its day-to-day functioning, the grand jury generally operates without the interference of a presiding judge.[25] It swears in its own witnesses[26], and deliberates in total secrecy.[27] We have insisted that the grand jury remain "free to pursue its investigations unhindered by external influence or supervision so long as it does not trench upon the legitimate rights of any witness called before it."[28] Recognizing this tradition of independence, we have said that the Fifth Amendment's 'constitutional guarantee presupposes an investigative body 'acting independently of either prosecuting attorney or judge'" [29]

THE FOX AND THE HEN HOUSE

"If the government can select the jurors, it will, of course, select those whom it supposes will be favorable to its enactments [like they do now]. And an exclusion of any of the freemen from eligibility is a selection of those not excluded [like they do now]. It will be seen, from the statutes cited, that the most absolute authority over the jury box that is, over the right of the people to sit in juries has been usurped by the government;" – Lysander Spooner, Trial by Jury, page 92, 1852.

In conclusion, the Jury has the unalienable right to consent, or not to consent, as to the government's accusations against the People. "The

---

[25] See Calandra, supra, 414 U.S., at 343, 94 S.Ct., at 617.
[26] Fed.Rule Crim.Proc. 6(c).
[27] United States v. Sells Engineering, Inc., 463 U.S., at 424-425, 103 S.Ct., at 3138.
[28] United States v. Dionisio, 410 U.S. 1, 17-18, 93 S.Ct. 764, 773, 35 L.Ed.2d 67 (1973).
[29] Id., at 16, 93 S.Ct., at 773 (emphasis added) (quoting Stirone, supra, 361 U.S., at 218, 80 S.Ct., at 273).

jury shall have the right to determine the law and the fact"[30] and the remedy/penalty and the power of Nullification.

KENTUCKY RESOLUTIONS

A series of resolutions drawn up by Jefferson, and adopted by the legislature of Kentucky in 1799, protesting against the "alien and sedition laws," declaring their illegality, announcing the strict constructionist theory of the federal government, and declaring "nullification" to be "the rightful remedy."

ORIGIN AND HISTORY OF THE GRAND JURY

The grand jury has a long and honorable tradition. It was recognized in the Magna Carta, the first English constitutional document, which King John accepted in 1215 at the demand of his subjects. The first English grand jury consisted of twenty five men selected from the knights or other freemen, who were summoned to inquire into crimes alleged to have been committed in their local community. Thus, grand jurors originally functioned as accusers or witnesses, rather than as judges.

Over the years, the hallmarks of our modern grand jury developed in England. For example, grand jury proceedings became secret, and the grand jury became independent of the Crown. As a result, a grand jury is able to vote an indictment or refuse to do so, as it deems proper, without regard to the recommendations of judge, prosecutor, or

---

[30] NY Constitution ARTICLE I - BILL OF RIGHTS §8.

any other person. This independence from the will of the government was achieved only after a long hard fight. It can best be illustrated by the celebrated English case involving the Earl of Shaftesbury, who, in 1681, fell under the suspicion of the Crown. Displeased with him, the Crown presented to the grand jury a proposed bill of indictment for high treason and recommended that it be voted and returned. After hearing the witnesses, the grand jury voted against the bill of indictment and returned it to the King, holding that it was not true.

When the English colonists came to America, they brought with them many of the institutions of the English legal system, including the grand jury. Thus, the English tradition of the common law grand jury was well established in the American colonies long before the American Revolution. Indeed, the colonists used it as a platform from which to assert their independence from the pressures of colonial governors. In 1735, for example, the Colonial Governor of New York demanded that a grand jury indict John Zenger, editor of a newspaper called "The Weekly Journal," for libel because he had held up to scorn certain acts of the Royal Governor. The grand jury flatly refused.

The grand jury as an institution was so firmly established in the traditions of our forebears that they included it in the Bill of Rights. The Fifth Amendment to the Constitution of the United States provides in part that "*no person shall be held to answer for a capital, or otherwise infamous crime, unless on a presentment or indictment of a Grand Jury . . . .*" Moreover, the grand jury system is also recognized in the constitutions of many of the states of the Union.

COMMON LAW

Common law is not statutes as distinguished from ecclesiastical law. It is the system of jurisprudence administered by the purely secular tribunals. Common law as distinguished from law created by the enactment of legislators, the common law comprises the body of those principles and rules of action, relating to the government and security of persons and property, which derive their authority solely from usages and customs of immemorial antiquity, or from the judgments and decrees of the courts recognizing, affirming, and enforcing such usages and customs; and, in this sense, particularly the ancient unwritten law of England.[31]

When the colonies separated from England, King John retaliated by revoking the charters. Technically, the colonies were without any legal authority to operate. However, civics (the branch of political philosophy concerned with individual rights) was generally taught and known by the people who asserted their rights and maintained order by applying the common law. The people united in the form of common law grand juries and continued the functioning of government.

"The Constitution for the United States of America acknowledges the Peoples' right to the common law of England as it was in 1789. What is that common law? It does not consist of absolute, fixed and inflexible rules; but, broad and comprehensive principles based on justice,

---

[31] 1 Kent, Comm. 492. Western Union Tel. Co. v. Call Pub. Co., 21 S.Ct. 561, 181 U.S. 92, 45 L.Ed. 765; Barry v. Port Jervis, 72 N.Y.S. 104, 64 App. Div. 268; U. S. v. Miller, D.C.Wash., 236 F. 798, 800.

reason, and common sense..."³² All state constitutions acknowledge the common law as the ultimate law system. Statutes and codes are applied only upon elected, appointed, and employed government individuals and people engaged in commercial activities. Statutes and codes are not to be applied upon the people.

Common Law a/k/a Natural Law is also the Magna Carta,³³ as authorized by the Confirmatio Cartarum, if the accused so demands.³⁴ The Confirmatio Cartarum succinctly says, *"our justices, sheriffs, mayors, and other ministers, which, under us have the laws of our land to guide, shall allow the said charters pleaded before them, in judgment in all their points; that is, to wit, the Great Charter as the common law and the Charter of the forest, for the wealth of our realm."*³⁵ In other words, the King's men must allow the Magna Carta to be pleaded as the common law if the accused so wishes it.

COMMON LAW ELUDES DEFINITION because it is NOT a list of laws; it is NOT built upon precedents or a collection of equity (*legislative law*) court rulings. Common Law is written into our hearts and minds being naturally common onto all men.

"This is the covenant that I will make with them after those days, saith the Lord, I will put my laws into their hearts, and in their minds will I write them." Heb 10:16

"For when the Gentiles, which have not the law, do by nature the things contained in the law, these, having not the law, are a law unto themselves: Which show the work of the law

---

³² Miller v. Monsen, 37 N.W.2d 543, 547, 228 Minn. 400.
³³ June 15, 1215, King John I.
³⁴ November 5, 1297, King Edward I.
³⁵ Confirmatio Cartarum, November 5, 1297.

written in their hearts, their conscience also bearing witness, and their thoughts the mean while accusing or else excusing one another." Rom 2:14-15

Common Law is the Laws of Nature and of Nature's God that proceeds upon two self-evident truths, called maxims: "For every injury there must be a remedy and in order, for there to be a crime there must be an injured party, without which no court may proceed."

Maxims are brief statements of self-evident truth that control our Common Law courts. They provided discernment in the writing of our founding documents. It is an adviser to our legislatures, and every consideration of mankind that seeks what's fair and best for all.

COURTS THAT DO NOT HONOR OR CONSIDER MAXIMS ARE NOT JUST

Indeed, whether and to what extent these common law maxims are honored by public leaders is how we test the way they administer the law to govern. Our courts were established to enforce these principles of common law, the word Justice is synonymous with virtue, and virtue is a biblical principle that emanates from Jesus Christ alone.[36] Maxims are the laws that never change. These statements set essential limits on truth and are essential to the fair and efficient

---

[36] Luke 6:17-19 And he came down with them, and stood in the plain, and the company of his disciples, and a great multitude of people out of all Judaea and Jerusalem, and from the sea coast of Tyre and Sidon, which came to hear him, and to be healed of their diseases; And they that were vexed with unclean spirits: and they were healed. And the whole multitude sought to touch him: for there went virtue out of him, and healed them all.

administration of justice according to the common law of mankind. No right-thinking person can disagree with a maxim. Every court is bound by the common law rules of equity established by the never-changing maxims. Maxims test those who judge and put an absolute limit on those who rule. Maxims[37] and precepts are the rules of common law. Maxims are self-evident truths used to adjudicate common law cases, axiom (sayings) in logic are self-evident indisputable truths, "the result of human reason and experience." Maxims are our common law heritage that binds us together as a people. If everyone knew the maxims of common law, our world would be a far better place.

THE FOLLOWING IS A SHORT LIST OF MAXIMS, A/K/A SELF-EVIDENT TRUTH

MAXIMS ON PRINCIPALS OF COMMON LAW
- All men are created equal.
- Men are endowed by their Creator with certain unalienable Rights.
- Liberty to all but preference to none.
- The safety of the people is the supreme law.
- The safety of the people cannot be judged but by the safety of every individual.
- To lie is to go against the mind.
- The only one who has any capacity or right or responsibility or knowledge to rebut your

---

[37] Maxims are but attempted general statements of rules of law and are law only to extent of application in adjudicated cases. Swetland v. Curtiss Airports Corporation, D.C.Ohio, 41 F. 2d 929, 936.; Coke defies a maxim to be "conclusion of reason," Co.Litt. 11a. He says in another place: "A maxim is a proposition to be of all men confessed and granted without proof, argument, or discourse." Id. 67a.

Affidavit of truth is the one who is adversely affected by it. It's his job, his right, his responsibility to speak for himself.
- No one else can know what your truth is or has the free-will responsibility to state it. This is YOUR job.
- Each of us is entitled to equal treatment under law.
- Workman is worthy of his hire.
- Nothing ventured, nothing gained.

MAXIMS ON THE LEGITIMACY OF GOVERNMENT:
- Just Governments derive their just powers from the consent of the governed.
- Unjust is State power where the law is either uncertain or unknown.
- The State should be subject to the law, for the law creates the State.
- The judge who decides a case without hearing both parties, though his decision be just, is himself unjust.
- Courts of justice are for the common people to command the power of the State.

MAXIMS ON TESTIMONY AND EVIDENCE:
- Words should be considered only as commonly understood and not with a meaning others construe to their own purpose.
- No one should be believed in court except upon his oath.
- Courts should not believe water runs upward of its own accord nor that impossibilities exist.
- The certainty of a thing in court arises only from making the thing certain in court.

MAXIMS ON CIVIC DUTY OF CITIZENS:
- Whenever any Form of Government becomes destructive, it is the Right of the People to alter or to abolish it, and to institute new Government.
- Each should use his own powers and property so as NOT to unjustly injure others.

MAXIMS ON PRIVATE PROPERTY:
- There is nothing more sacred, more inviolate, than the house of every citizen.
- Every home is a castle; though the winds of heaven blow through it, officers of the State cannot enter.
- Title is the right to enjoy possession of that which is our own.

MAXIMS ON UNALIENABLE RIGHTS:
- The Bill of Rights is a list of self-evident truths.
- None has a greater claim to live free.
- No one should be required to betray himself, i.e., no one should be made to testify against himself.
- The right of the People to keep and bear arms is necessary for the security of a free state.
- Everyone should be presumed innocent until his guilt is established beyond a reasonable doubt.
- Liberty to all but preference to none.
- None is entitled to any privilege denied to others ... absolutely none!
- It is against justness for freemen not to have the free disposal of their own property.
- No king, no priest, no celebrity, no judge, not any person has any greater right to walk free than any carpenter, plumber, or law-abiding street minstrel.

MAXIMS ON CRIME AND PUNISHMENT:
- He who acts in pure defense of his own life or limb is justified.
- Crimes are more effectually prevented by the certainty than by the severity of punishment.
- Perjured witnesses should be punished for perjury and for the crimes they falsely accuse against others.

MAXIMS ON JUDICIAL REASONING:
- The burden of proof lies on him who asserts the fact, not on him who denies it, because from the very nature of things a negative cannot be proof.
- No one should be twice harassed for the same offense.
- We are all equals in the sight of our law.
- Maxims test those who judge.
- Maxims put an absolute limit on those who rule.
- He who slices the pie should be last to take a piece.
- Servant judges cannot judge sovereigns.
- A thing similar is not exactly the same thing.
- Innocent until proven guilty.
- No one is above the law.
- Words should be considered only as commonly understood and not with a meaning others construe to their own purpose.
- All are equal under the law.
- Truth is expressed in the form of an affidavit.
- An unrebutted affidavit stands as truth.
- He who leaves the battlefield first loses by default.
- Sacrifice is the measure of credibility.
- A lien or claim can be satisfied only through rebuttable by affidavit point by point, resolution by jury, or payment.

- He who bears the burden ought also to derive the benefit.
- If the plaintiff does not prove his case, the defendant is absolved.
- No court and no judge can overturn or disregard or abrogate somebody's Affidavit of Truth.
- Words should be interpreted most strongly against him who uses them.

You can find Maxims of Law from Bouvier's 1856 Law Dictionary - The Lawful Path and Sir Edward Coke at www.nationallibertyalliance.org.

In conclusion, there are 1000's of Maxims and many yet to be discovered. They are simply pure logic and justness clearly seen by any reasonable person.

NATURE OF THE GRAND JURY

The powers and functions of the common law grand jury differ from those of the petit jury. The Grand jury listens to the evidence offered by the Sheriff or Coroner and the defense (if it chooses to offer any) and decides whether they believe that there is a crime and that the accused appears to be the perpetrator of that crime.

During a criminal trial the Petit Jury returns a verdict of guilty or not guilty. The grand jury, on the other hand, does not determine guilt or innocence, but only whether there is probable cause to believe that a crime was committed and that a specific person or persons committed it. If the grand jury finds probable cause to exist, then it will return a written statement of the charges called an "indictment." After that, the accused will go to trial.

The grand jury normally hears only that evidence presented by the Sheriff or the Coroner which tends to show the commission of a crime. The grand jury must determine from this evidence, and usually without hearing evidence for the defense, whether a person should be tried for a serious crime, referred to in the Bill of Rights as an "infamous crime."

An infamous crime is a crime potentially punishable by imprisonment, within the provision of the fifth amendment of the constitution that *"no person shall be held to answer for a capital or otherwise infamous crime unless on a presentment or indictment of a grand jury."*[38] It is not the character of the crime but the nature of the punishment which renders the crime "infamous."[39]

As a general rule, no one can be prosecuted for a serious crime unless the grand jury decides that the evidence it has heard so requires. In this way, the grand jury operates both as a "sword," authorizing the government's prosecution of suspected criminals, and also as a "shield," protecting citizens from unwarranted or inappropriate prosecutions.

THE GRAND JURY'S TASKS

As stated above, the grand jury's function is to determine whether a person shall be tried for a serious crime alleged to have been committed within the county or federal district where it sits.

---

[38] Mackin v. U. S., 117 U.S. 348, 6 S.Ct. 777, 29 L. Ed. 909; Brede v. Powers, 263 U.S. 4, 44 S.Ct. 8, 68 L.Ed. 132.

[39] Weeks v. United States, C.C.A.N.Y., 216 F. 292, 298, L.R.A. 1915B, 651. But see Drazen v. New Haven Taxicab Co., 95 Conn. 500, 111 A. 861, 864.

Matters may be brought to its attention by Sheriffs or Coroners, and from the personal knowledge of a member of the grand jury or from matters brought to a member's personal attention. In all these cases, the grand jury must hear evidence before taking action.

After it has received evidence against a person, the grand jury must decide whether the evidence presented justifies an indictment, or "true bill," which is the formal criminal charge returned by the grand jury.

If the evidence does not persuade the grand jury that there is probable cause to believe the person committed a crime, the grand jury will vote a "no bill," or "not a true bill."

INVESTIGATION

The major portion of the grand jury's work is concerned with evidence brought to its attention by the person bringing the charges. The grand jury may consider additional matters otherwise brought to its attention and may ask a Jury Administrator for assistance on how they might want to go forward.

SELECTION OF GRAND JURORS

A grand jury is selected at random from a fair cross section of the community in the county or federal district where the alleged crime occurred. Thus, all citizens have an equal opportunity and obligation to serve.

Pursuant to law, the names of prospective grand jurors are drawn at random from lists of registered voters or lists of actual voters, or other sources when necessary, under procedures designed to ensure that all groups in the community will have a fair chance to serve. Those persons whose names have been drawn and who are not exempt or excused from service are summoned to appear for duty as grand jurors.

When these persons appear before the court, the presiding magistrate may consider any further requests to be excused. The magistrate will then direct the selection of 25 qualified persons to become the members of the grand jury.

ORGANIZATION, OATH, AND OFFICERS

After the proper number of persons has been qualified as grand jurors, the Jury Administrator will appoint one of them to be the foreman, or presiding officer, of the grand jury. A deputy foreman will also be appointed, so that he or she can act as presiding officer in the foreman's absence. The foreman, the deputy foreman, and the remaining members of the grand jury are sworn in by the Clerk of the Court.

The oath taken by the grand jurors binds them to inquire diligently and objectively into all crimes committed within the district of which they have or may obtain evidence and to conduct such inquiry without malice, fear, hatred, or other emotion.

After the grand jurors have been sworn, the Jury Administrator will orientate and advises the grand jury of its obligations and how best to perform its duties. Careful attention must be paid to the instructions that may be given. After orientation the grand jury will hear testimony and consider documentary evidence in the cases brought to its attention.

Procedure

1) <u>Quorum</u>: Thirteen of the 25 members of the grand jury constitute a quorum for the transaction of business. If fewer than thirteen are present, even for a moment, the proceedings of the grand jury must stop. This shows how important it is that each grand juror conscientiously attends the meetings. If an emergency will prevent a grand juror's attendance at the meeting, he or she must promptly advise the grand jury foreman. If the juror's absence will prevent the grand jury from acting, the grand juror should, if at all possible, attend the meeting.

2) <u>Evidence before the Grand Jury</u>: Much of the grand jury's time is spent hearing testimony by witnesses and examining documentary or other evidence in order to determine whether such evidence justifies an indictment. The grand jury may ask that additional witnesses be called if it believes this necessary. The Jury Administrator will also assist in the preparation of the formal written indictments that the grand jury wishes to present. But no one other than the grand jury may remain in the room while the grand jury deliberates and votes on an indictment.

3) <u>Questioning the Witness</u>: Witnesses are called to testify one after another. Upon appearing to give testimony, each witness will be sworn by the grand jury foreman or, in the foreman's absence, the deputy foreman. The witness will then be questioned. Ordinarily, the prosecuting person for the government questions the witness first, followed next by the foreman of the grand jury. Then, the other

members of the grand jury may question the witness.

All questions asked of each witness must be relevant and proper, relating only to the case under investigation. If doubt should arise as to whether a question is appropriate, the advice of the Jury Administrator may be sought. If necessary, a ruling may be obtained from the court.

Because of the need for secrecy, described in more detail in the following section, the law forbids anyone other than authorized persons from being present in the grand jury room while evidence is being presented. This means that only the grand jury, the Jury Administrator, those prosecuting, the witness under examination, the court reporter, and interpreters when needed may be present.

Occasionally, prior to answering a question, a witness may ask to leave the grand jury room to consult with his or her attorney. The grand jury is to draw no adverse inference from such conduct, for every witness has the right to confer with counsel even though counsel may not be present in the grand jury room.

In fact, a witness may confer with counsel after each question, as long as he or she does not make a mockery of the proceedings or does not, by such, make an attempt to impede the orderly progress of the grand jury investigation.

Additionally, a witness who is appearing before the grand jury may invoke the Fifth Amendment privilege against self-incrimination and refuse to answer a question. In such a situation, the grand jurors may bring the matter before the court in order to obtain a ruling as to whether or not the answer may be compelled. One manner in which an answer may be compelled is by granting the witness immunity from prosecution in exchange for the witness' testimony.

4) CALLING THE PERSON UNDER INVESTIGATION AS A WITNESS: Normally, neither the person under investigation (sometimes referred to as the "accused," although this does not imply he or she is guilty of any crime) nor any witness on the accused's behalf will testify before the grand jury.

Upon request, preferably in writing, an accused may be given the opportunity by the grand jury to appear before it. An accused that does so appear cannot be forced to testify because of the constitutional privilege against self-incrimination.

If the grand jury attempts to force the accused to testify, an indictment returned against that person may be nullified.

Because the appearance of an accused before the grand jury may raise complicated legal problems, a grand jury that desires to request or to permit an accused to appear before it should consult with the United States Attorney and, if necessary, the court before proceeding.

Even if the accused is willing to testify voluntarily, it is recommended that he or she first be warned of the right not to testify. Also, he or she may be required to sign a formal waiver of this right. The grand jury should be completely satisfied that the accused fully understands what he or she is doing.

5) <u>THE EVIDENCE NEEDED BEFORE A "TRUE BILL" MAY BE VOTED</u>: It is the responsibility of the grand jury to weigh the evidence presented to it in order to determine whether this evidence, usually without any explanation being offered by the accused, persuades it that there is probable cause to believe that a crime has been committed and that the accused was the person who committed it.

   Remember that the grand jury is not responsible for determining whether the accused is guilty beyond a reasonable doubt, but only whether there is sufficient evidence of probable cause to justify bringing the accused to trial. Only the evidence presented to the grand jury in the grand jury room may be considered in determining whether to vote an indictment.

6) <u>DELIBERATIONS</u>: When the grand jury has received all the evidence on a given charge, all persons other than the members of the grand jury or an interpreter to assist a juror who is hearing or speech impaired, must leave the room so that the grand jury may begin its deliberations. The presence of any other person in the grand jury room while the grand jury deliberates or votes may nullify an indictment returned on the accusation.

   After all persons other than the grand jury members and any interpreter for a hearing or speech impaired juror have left the room, the foreman will ask the grand jury members to discuss and vote upon the question of whether the evidence persuades the grand jury that a crime has probably been committed by the person accused and that an indictment should be returned. Every grand juror has the right to express his or her view of the matter under consideration, and grand jurors should listen to the comments of all their fellow grand jurors before making up their mind. Only after each grand juror has been given the opportunity to be heard will the vote be taken. It should be remembered that at least 13 jurors must be present and 12 members must vote in favor of the indictment before it may be returned.

The foreman of the grand jury must keep a record of the number of jurors concurring in the finding of every indictment and file the record with the Clerk of the Court. If an indictment is found, the grand jury will report it to the judge or a magistrate judge in open court. It will likewise report any "not true bills," or decisions not to indict. A decision not to indict should immediately be reported to the court in writing by the foreman so that the accused may promptly be released from jail or freed from bail.

SECRECY

The law imposes upon each grand juror a strict obligation of secrecy. This obligation is emphasized in the oath each grand juror takes and in the charge given to the grand jury by the judge.

The tradition of secrecy continues as a vital part of the grand jury system for many reasons. It protects the grand jurors from being subjected to pressure by persons who may be subjects of investigations by the grand jury or associates of such persons. It prevents the escape of those against whom an indictment is being considered. It encourages witnesses before the grand jury to give full and truthful information as to the commission of a crime. It also prevents tampering with or intimidation of such witnesses before they testify at trial.

Finally, it prevents the disclosure of investigations that result in no action by the grand jury and avoids any stigma the public might attach to one who is the subject of a mere investigation by the grand jury.

Essentially, the grand jury may disclose matters occurring before it only to the Sheriff and/or Jury Administrator for use in the performance of their duties, but even the Sheriff and Jury Administrator may not be informed of what took place during the grand jury's deliberations and voting. The only other time matters occurring before the grand jury may be disclosed to anyone is when disclosure is ordered by the court in the interests of justice. Disclosure of such matters may never be made to grand juror's friends or family, including a grand juror's spouse.

PROTECTION OF GRAND JURORS

The secrecy imposed upon grand jurors is a major source of protection for them. In addition, no inquiry may be made to learn what grand jurors said or how they voted, except upon order of the court.

The law gives the members of a grand jury broad immunity for actions taken by them within the scope of their authority as grand jurors. Because of this immunity, all grand jurors must perform their duties with the highest sense of responsibility.

Practical Suggestions For Grand Jurors

- Each juror should attend the grand jury sessions regularly, in order to ensure that a quorum of 13 members will be present to conduct the grand jury's business.
- Each juror should be on time for each meeting so that others are not kept waiting. The time of meetings should be scheduled so as to be convenient for the grand jury, the Sheriff, and the witnesses. Witnesses should be treated courteously when they appear before the grand jury. Questions should be put to them in an orderly fashion. The Sheriff should complete his or her questioning of each witness before the foreman asks questions. The remaining grand jurors will then have a chance to ask relevant and proper questions.
- Each juror has an equal voice in determining whether or not an indictment should be returned. Therefore, it is important that all grand jurors pay close attention to the testimony and other evidence presented.
- Each juror must be absolutely fair in his or her judgment of the facts. Otherwise, the grand juror will defeat the purpose the grand jury is designed to serve.
- During deliberations on a case, each grand juror should feel free to express his or her opinion based upon the evidence.
- Each juror has equal duties and responsibilities, and each is entitled to be satisfied with the evidence before being called upon to vote. No juror has the right to dismiss a witness or to shut off proper discussion if other jurors wish to pursue the matter further.

- No jury should undertake to investigate matters outside its proper scope merely because someone suggested an investigation, or because the investigation would be interesting.
- No juror should discuss the cases under investigation with anyone, except fellow grand jurors and the Sheriff and then only in the grand jury room. Of course, the grand jurors may always seek the advice of the Jury Administrator.
- Finally, every citizen who is selected to serve on a federal grand jury should bring to this task the determination to participate in a responsible manner and to make every effort to ensure that the grand jury will be a credit not only to the community it represents but to the United States.

JURIST VOW

I vow[40] to the Governor of the Universe, in my capacity as Jurist, to insure that all public servants uphold the Declaration of Independence, US Constitution and Bill of Rights; and to carry out all of my deliberating under Natural Law; principled under Justice, Honor, and Mercy; And to strictly adhere to the following two legal maxims: (1) Every right when with-held must have a remedy, and every injury it's proper redress, and (2) In the absence of a victim there can be no crime "corpus delecti"; the State cannot be the victim but the People of the state can be.

---

[40] Num 30:2 If a man vow a vow unto the LORD, or swear an oath to bind his soul with a bond; he shall not break his word, he shall do according to all that proceedeth out of his mouth.

GLOSSARY OF TERMS

- **Accused:** The person accused of the commission of a crime. Use of this term does not imply the person under investigation is guilty of any crime. After a person is indicted by the grand jury, that person is referred to as the "defendant."
- **Charge to the Grand Jury:** Given by the Jury Administrator presiding over the selection and organization of the grand jury, the charge is the court's instructions to the grand jury as to its duties, functions, and obligations, and how to best perform them.
- **Deliberations:** The discussion by the grand jury members as to whether or not to return an indictment on a given charge against an accused. During deliberations no one except the grand jury members or an interpreter for a hearing or speech impaired juror may be present.
- **District:** The geographical area over which a federal district court where the grand jury sits and the grand jury itself have jurisdiction. The territorial limitations of the district will be explained to the grand jury by the district judge.
- **Evidence:** Testimony of witnesses, documents, and exhibits as presented to the grand jury by the Sheriff or otherwise properly brought before it. In some instances, the person under investigation may also testify.
- **Federal:** The national government as distinguished from the state governments.
- **Grand Jurors' Immunity:** Immunity is granted to all grand jurors for their authorized actions while serving on a grand jury and means that no grand juror may be penalized for actions

taken within the scope of his or her service as a grand juror.

- **Indictment:** The written formal charge of a crime by the grand jury, returned when 12 or more grand jurors vote in favor of it.
- **Information:** The written formal charge of crime by the prosecutor to the Sheriff, filed against an accused who, if charged with a serious crime, must have knowingly waived the requirements that the evidence first be presented to a grand jury.
- **"No Bill":** Also referred to as "not a true bill," the "no bill" is the decision by the grand jury not to indict a person.
- **Petit Jury:** The trial jury composed of 12 members that hear a case after indictment and renders a verdict or decision after hearing the prosecution's entire case and whatever evidence the defendant chooses to offer.
- **Probable Cause:** The finding necessary in order to return an indictment against a person accused of a crime. A finding of probable cause is proper only when the evidence presented to the grand jury, without any explanation being offered by the accused, persuades 12 or more grand jurors that a crime has probably been committed by the person accused.

BILL OF RIGHTS

AMENDMENT I: Congress shall make no law respecting an establishment of religion, or prohibiting the free exercise thereof; or abridging the freedom of speech, or of the press; or the right of the people peaceably to assemble, and to Grandion the Government for a redress of grievances.

AMENDMENT II: A well regulated Militia, being necessary to the security of a free State, the right of the people to keep and bear Arms, shall not be infringed.

AMENDMENT III: No Soldier shall, in time of peace be quartered in any house, without the consent of the Owner, nor in time of war, but in a manner to be prescribed by law.

AMENDMENT IV: The right of the people to be secure in their persons, houses, papers, and effects, against unreasonable searches and seizures, shall not be violated, and no Warrants shall issue, but upon probable cause, supported by Oath or affirmation, and particularly describing the place to be searched, and the persons or things to be seized.

AMENDMENT V: No person shall be held to answer for a capital, or otherwise infamous crime, unless on a presentment or indictment of a Grand Jury, except in cases arising in the land or naval forces, or in the Militia, when in actual service in time of War or public danger; nor shall any person be subject for the same offence to be twice put in jeopardy of life or limb; nor shall be compelled in any criminal case to be a witness against himself, nor be deprived of life, liberty, or property, without due process of law; nor shall private property be taken for public use, without just compensation.

AMENDMENT VI: In all criminal prosecutions, the accused shall enjoy the right to a speedy and public trial, by an impartial jury of the State and district wherein the crime shall have been committed, which district shall have been previously ascertained by law, and to be informed of the nature and cause of the accusation; to be confronted with the witnesses against him; to have compulsory process for obtaining witnesses in his favor, and to have the Assistance of Counsel for his defense.

AMENDMENT VII: In suits at common law, where the value in controversy shall exceed twenty dollars, the right of trial by jury shall be preserved, and no fact tried by a jury, shall be otherwise reexamined in any Court of the United States, than according to the rules of the common law.

AMENDMENT VIII: Excessive bail shall not be required, nor excessive fines imposed, nor cruel and unusual punishments inflicted.

AMENDMENT IX: The enumeration in the Constitution, of certain rights, shall not be construed to deny or disparage others retained by the people.

AMENDMENT X: The powers not delegated to the United States by the Constitution, nor prohibited by it to the States, ARE RESERVED TO THE STATES RESPECTIVELY, OR TO THE PEOPLE.

THE DECLARATION OF INDEPENDENCE IN CONGRESS, JULY 4, 1776

The unanimous Declaration of the thirteen united States of America, When in the Course of human events, it becomes necessary for one people to dissolve the political bands which have connected them with another, and to assume among the powers of the earth, the separate and equal station to which the Laws of Nature and of Nature's God entitle them, a decent respect to the opinions of mankind requires that they should declare the causes which impel them to the separation.

We hold these truths to be self-evident, that all men are created equal, that they are endowed by their Creator with certain unalienable Rights, that among these are Life, Liberty and the pursuit of Happiness. -- That to secure these rights, Governments are instituted among Men, deriving their just powers from the consent of the governed, -- That whenever any Form of Government becomes destructive of these ends, it is the Right of the People to alter or to abolish it, and to institute new Government, laying its foundation on such principles and organizing its powers in such form, as to them shall seem most likely to affect their Safety and Happiness. Prudence, indeed, will dictate that Governments long established should not be changed for light and transient causes; and accordingly all experience hath shewn, that mankind are more disposed to suffer, while evils are sufferable, than to right themselves by abolishing the forms to which they are accustomed. But when a long train of abuses and usurpations, pursuing invariably the same Object evinces a design to reduce them under absolute Despotism, it is their right, it is their duty, to throw off such Government, and to provide new Guards for their future security.-- Such has been the patient sufferance of these Colonies; and such is now the necessity which constrains them to alter their former Systems of Government. The history of the present King of Great Britain is a history of repeated injuries and usurpations, all having in direct object the establishment of an absolute Tyranny over these States. To prove this, let Facts be submitted to a candid world.

He has refused his Assent to Laws, the most wholesome and necessary for the public good.

He has forbidden his Governors to pass Laws of immediate and pressing importance, unless suspended in their operation till his Assent should be obtained; and when so suspended, he has utterly neglected to attend to them.

He has refused to pass other Laws for the accommodation of large districts of people, unless those people would relinquish the right of Representation in the Legislature, a right inestimable to them and formidable to tyrants only.

He has called together legislative bodies at places unusual, uncomfortable, and distant from the depository of their public Records, for the sole purpose of fatiguing them into compliance with his measures.

He has dissolved Representative Houses repeatedly, for opposing with manly firmness his invasions on the rights of the people.

He has refused for a long time, after such dissolutions, to cause others to be elected; whereby the Legislative powers, incapable of Annihilation, have returned to the People at large for their exercise; the State remaining in the meantime exposed to all the dangers of invasion from without, and convulsions within.

He has endeavored to prevent the population of these States; for that purpose obstructing the Laws for Naturalization of Foreigners; refusing to pass others to encourage their migrations hither, and raising the conditions of new Appropriations of Lands.

He has obstructed the Administration of Justice, by refusing his Assent to Laws for establishing Judiciary powers.

He has made Judges dependent on his Will alone, for the tenure of their offices, and the amount and payment of their salaries.

He has erected a multitude of New Offices, and sent hither swarms of Officers to harass our people, and eat out their substance.

He has kept among us, in times of peace, Standing Armies without the Consent of our legislatures.

He has affected to render the Military independent of and superior to the Civil power.

He has combined with others to subject us to a jurisdiction foreign to our constitution, and unacknowledged by our laws; giving his Assent to their Acts of pretended Legislation:

For quartering large bodies of armed troops among us:

For protecting them, by a mock Trial, from punishment for any Murders which they should commit on the Inhabitants of these States:

For cutting off our Trade with all parts of the world:

For imposing Taxes on us without our Consent:

For depriving us in many cases, of the benefits of Trial by Jury:

For transporting us beyond Seas to be tried for pretended offences

For abolishing the free System of English Laws in a neighboring Province, establishing therein an arbitrary government, and enlarging its Boundaries so as to render it at once an example and fit instrument for introducing the same absolute rule into these Colonies:

For taking away our Charters, abolishing our most valuable Laws, and altering fundamentally the Forms of our Governments:

For suspending our own Legislatures and declaring themselves invested with power to legislate for us in all cases whatsoever.

He has abdicated Government here, by declaring us out of his Protection and waging War against us.

He has plundered our seas, ravaged our Coasts, burnt our towns, and destroyed the lives of our people.

He is at this time transporting large Armies of foreign Mercenaries to complete the works of death, desolation and tyranny, already begun with circumstances of Cruelty & perfidy scarcely paralleled in the most barbarous ages, and totally unworthy the Head of a civilized nation.

He has constrained our fellow Citizens taken Captive on the high Seas to bear Arms against their Country, to become the executioners of their friends and Brethren, or to fall themselves by their Hands.

He has excited domestic insurrections amongst us, and has endeavored to bring on the inhabitants of our frontiers, the merciless Indian Savages, whose known rule of warfare, is an undistinguished destruction of all ages, sexes and conditions.

In every stage of these Oppressions We have Petitioned for Redress in the most humble terms: Our repeated Petitions have been answered only by repeated injury. A Prince whose character is thus marked by every act which may define a Tyrant, is unfit to be the ruler of a free people.

Nor have We been wanting in attentions to our British brethren. We have warned them from time to time of attempts by their legislature to extend an unwarrantable jurisdiction over us. We have reminded them of the circumstances of our emigration and settlement here. We have appealed to their native justice and magnanimity, and we have conjured them by the ties of our common kindred to disavow these usurpations, which would inevitably interrupt our connections and correspondence. They too have been deaf to the voice of justice and of consanguinity. We must, therefore, acquiesce in the necessity, which denounces our Separation, and hold them, as we hold the rest of mankind, Enemies in War, in Peace Friends.

We, therefore, the Representatives of the united States of America, in General Congress, Assembled, appealing to the Supreme Judge of the world for the rectitude of our intentions, do, in the Name, and by Authority of the good People of these Colonies, solemnly publish and declare, That these United Colonies are, and of Right ought to be Free and Independent States; that they are Absolved from all Allegiance to the British Crown, and that all political connection between them and the State of Great Britain, is and ought to be totally dissolved; and that as Free and Independent States, they have full Power to levy War, conclude Peace, contract Alliances, establish Commerce, and to do all other Acts and Things which Independent States may of right do. And for the support of this Declaration, with a firm reliance on the protection of divine Providence, we mutually pledge to each other our Lives, our Fortunes and our sacred Honor.

The 56 signatures on the Declaration appear in the positions indicated:

[Column 1]
Georgia:
Button Gwinnett
Lyman Hall
George Walton

[Column 2]
North Carolina:
William Hooper
Joseph Hewes
John Penn
South Carolina:
Edward Rutledge
Thomas Heyward, Jr.
Thomas Lynch, Jr.
Arthur Middleton

[Column 3]
Massachusetts:
John Hancock
Maryland:
Samuel Chase
William Paca
Thomas Stone
Charles Carroll of Carrollton
Virginia:
George Wythe
Richard Henry Lee
Thomas Jefferson
Benjamin Harrison
Thomas Nelson, Jr.
Francis Lightfoot Lee
Carter Braxton

[Column 4]
Pennsylvania:
Robert Morris
Benjamin Rush
Benjamin Franklin
John Morton
George Clymer
James Smith
George Taylor
James Wilson
George Ross
Delaware:
Caesar Rodney
George Read
Thomas McKean

[Column 5]
New York:
William Floyd
Philip Livingston
Francis Lewis
Lewis Morris
New Jersey:
Richard Stockton
John Witherspoon
Francis Hopkinson
John Hart
Abraham Clark

[Column 6]
New Hampshire:
Josiah Bartlett
William Whipple
Massachusetts:
Samuel Adams
John Adams
Robert Treat Paine
Elbridge Gerry
Rhode Island:
Stephen Hopkins
William Ellery
Connecticut:
Roger Sherman
Samuel Huntington
William Williams
Oliver Wolcott
New Hampshire:
Matthew Thornton

THE CONSTITUTION FOR THE UNITED STATES

We the people of the United States, in order to form a more perfect union, establish justice, insure domestic tranquility, provide for the common defense, promote the general welfare, and secure the blessings of liberty to ourselves and our posterity, do ordain and establish this Constitution for the United States of America.

Article I LEGISLATIVE POWERS

Section 1: ALL LEGISLATIVE POWERS herein granted shall be vested in a Congress of the United States, which shall consist of a Senate and House of Representatives.

Section 2: THE HOUSE OF REPRESENTATIVES shall be composed of members chosen every second year by the people of the several states, and the electors in each state shall have the qualifications requisite for electors of the most numerous branch of the state legislature.

No person shall be a Representative who shall not have attained to the age of twenty five years, and been seven years a citizen of the United States, and who shall not, when elected, be an inhabitant of that state in which he shall be chosen.

Representatives and direct taxes shall be apportioned among the several states which may be included within this union, according to their respective numbers, which shall be determined by adding to the whole number of free persons, including those bound to service for a term of years, and excluding Indians not taxed, three fifths of all other Persons. The actual Enumeration shall be made within three years after the first meeting of the Congress of the United States, and within every subsequent term of ten years, in such manner as they shall by law direct. The number of Representatives shall not exceed one for every thirty thousand, but each state shall have at least one Representative; and until such enumeration shall be made, the state of New Hampshire shall be entitled to chuse three, Massachusetts eight, Rhode Island and Providence Plantations one, Connecticut five, New York six, New Jersey four, Pennsylvania eight, Delaware one, Maryland six, Virginia ten, North Carolina five, South Carolina five, and Georgia three.

When vacancies happen in the Representation from any state, the executive authority thereof shall issue writs of election to fill such vacancies. The House of Representatives shall choose their speaker and other officers; and shall have the sole power of impeachment.

Section 3: THE SENATE OF THE UNITED STATES shall be composed of two Senators from each state, chosen by the legislature thereof, for six years; and each Senator shall have one vote.

Immediately after they shall be assembled in consequence of the first election, they shall be divided as equally as may be into three classes. The seats of the Senators of the first class shall be vacated at the expiration of the second year, of the second class at the expiration of the fourth year, and the third class at the expiration of the sixth year, so that one third may be chosen every second year; and if vacancies happen by resignation, or otherwise, during the recess of the legislature of any state, the executive thereof may make temporary appointments until the next meeting of the legislature, which shall then fill such vacancies.

No person shall be a Senator who shall not have attained to the age of thirty years, and been nine years a citizen of the United States and who shall not, when elected, be an inhabitant of that state for which he shall be chosen.

The Vice President of the United States shall be President of the Senate, but shall have no vote, unless they be equally divided.

The Senate shall choose their other officers, and also a President pro tempore, in the absence of the Vice
President, or when he shall exercise the office of President of the United States.

The Senate shall have the sole power to try all impeachments. When sitting for that purpose, they shall be on oath or affirmation. When the President of the United States is tried, the Chief Justice shall preside: And no person shall be convicted without the concurrence of two thirds of the members present.

Judgment in cases of impeachment shall not extend further than to removal from office, and disqualification to hold and enjoy any office of honor, trust or profit under the United States: but the party convicted shall nevertheless be liable and subject to indictment, trial, judgment and punishment, according to law.

Section 4: The times, places and manner of holding elections for Senators and Representatives, shall be prescribed in each state by the legislature thereof; but the Congress may at any time by law make or alter such regulations, except as to the places of choosing Senators.

The Congress shall assemble at least once in every year, and such meeting shall be on the first Monday in December, unless they shall by law appoint a different day.

Section 5: Each House shall be the judge of the elections, returns and qualifications of its own members, and a majority of each shall constitute a quorum to do business; but a smaller number may adjourn from day to day, and may be authorized to compel the attendance of absent members, in such manner, and under such penalties as each House may provide.

Each House may determine the rules of its proceedings, punish its members for disorderly behavior, and, with the concurrence of two thirds, expel a member.

Each House shall keep a journal of its proceedings, and from time to time publish the same, excepting such parts as may in their judgment require secrecy; and the yeas and nays of the members of either House on any question shall, at the desire of one fifth of those present, be entered on the journal.

Neither House, during the session of Congress, shall, without the consent of the other, adjourn for more than three days, nor to any other place than that in which the two Houses shall be sitting.

Section 6: The Senators and Representatives shall receive a compensation for their services, to be ascertained by law, and paid out of the treasury of the United States. They shall in all cases, except treason, felony and breach of the peace, be privileged from arrest during their attendance at the session of their respective Houses, and in going to and returning from the same; and for any speech or debate in either House, they shall not be questioned in any other place.

No Senator or Representative shall, during the time for which he was elected, be appointed to any civil office under the authority of the United States, which shall have been created, or the emoluments whereof shall have been increased during such time: and no person holding any office under the United States, shall be a member of either House during his continuance in office.

Section 7: All bills for raising revenue shall originate in the House of Representatives; but the Senate may
propose or concur with amendments as on other Bills.

Every bill which shall have passed the House of Representatives and the Senate, shall, before it become a law, be presented to the President of the United States; if he approve he shall sign it, but if not he shall return it, with his objections to that House in which it shall have originated, who shall enter the objections at large on their journal, and proceed to reconsider it. If after such reconsideration two thirds of that House shall agree to pass the bill, it shall be sent, together with the objections, to the other House, by which it shall likewise be reconsidered, and if approved by two thirds of that House, it shall become a law. But in all such cases the votes of both Houses shall be determined by yeas and nays, and the names of the persons voting for and against the bill shall be entered on the journal of each House respectively. If any bill shall not be returned by the President within ten days (Sundays excepted) after it shall have been presented to him, the same shall be a law, in like manner as if he had signed it, unless the Congress by their adjournment prevent its return, in which case it shall not be a law.

Every order, resolution, or vote to which the concurrence of the Senate and House of Representatives may be necessary (except on a question of adjournment) shall be presented to the President of the United States; and before the same shall take effect, shall be approved by him, or being disapproved by him, shall be repassed by two thirds of the Senate and House of Representatives, according to the rules and limitations prescribed in the case of a bill.

Section 8: The Congress shall have power to lay and collect taxes, duties, imposts and excises, to pay the debts and provide for the common defense and general welfare of the United States; but all duties, imposts and excises shall be uniform throughout the United States;

To borrow money on the credit of the United States;

To regulate commerce with foreign nations, and among the several states, and with the Indian tribes;

To establish a uniform rule of naturalization, and uniform laws on the subject of bankruptcies throughout the United States;

To coin money, regulate the value thereof, and of foreign coin, and fix the standard of weights and measures;

To provide for the punishment of counterfeiting the securities and current coin of the United States;

To establish post offices and post roads;

To promote the progress of science and useful arts, by securing for limited times to authors and inventors the exclusive right to their respective writings and discoveries;

To constitute tribunals inferior to the Supreme Court;

To define and punish piracies and felonies committed on the high seas, and offenses against the law of nations;

To declare war, grant letters of marque and reprisal, and make rules concerning captures on land and water;

To raise and support armies, but no appropriation of money to that use shall be for a longer term than two years;

To provide and maintain a navy;

To make rules for the government and regulation of the land and naval forces;

To provide for calling forth the militia to execute the laws of the union, suppress insurrections and repel invasions;

To provide for organizing, arming, and disciplining, the militia, and for governing such part of them as may be employed in the service of the United States, reserving to the states respectively, the appointment of the officers, and the authority of training the militia according to the discipline prescribed by Congress;

To exercise exclusive legislation in all cases whatsoever, over such District (not exceeding ten miles square) as may, by cession of particular states, and the acceptance of Congress, become the seat of the government of the United States, and to exercise like authority over all places purchased by the consent of the legislature of the state in which the same shall be, for the erection of forts, magazines, arsenals, dockyards, and other needful buildings;--And

To make all laws which shall be necessary and proper for carrying into execution the foregoing powers, and all other powers vested by this Constitution in the government of the United States, or in any department or officer thereof.

Section 9: The migration or importation of such persons as any of the states now existing shall think proper to admit, shall not be prohibited by the Congress prior to the year one thousand eight hundred and eight, but a tax or duty may be imposed on such importation, not exceeding ten dollars for each person.

The privilege of the writ of habeas corpus shall not be suspended, unless when in cases of rebellion or invasion the public safety may require it.

No bill of attainder or ex post facto Law shall be passed.

No capitation, or other direct, tax shall be laid, unless in proportion to the census or enumeration herein before directed to be taken.

No tax or duty shall be laid on articles exported from any state.

No preference shall be given by any regulation of commerce or revenue to the ports of one state over those of another: nor shall vessels bound to, or from, one state, be obliged to enter, clear or pay duties in another.

No money shall be drawn from the treasury, but in consequence of appropriations made by law; and a regular statement and account of receipts and expenditures of all public money shall be published from time to time.

No title of nobility shall be granted by the United States: and no person holding any office of profit or trust
under them, shall, without the consent of the Congress, accept of any present, emolument, office, or title, of any kind whatever, from any king, prince, or foreign state.

Section 10: No state shall enter into any treaty, alliance, or confederation; grant letters of marque and reprisal; coin money; emit bills of credit; make anything but gold and silver coin a tender in payment of debts; pass any bill of attainder, ex post facto law, or law impairing the obligation of contracts, or grant any title of nobility.

No state shall, without the consent of the Congress, lay any imposts or duties on imports or exports, except what may be absolutely necessary for executing its inspection laws: and the net produce of all duties and imposts, laid by any state on imports or exports, shall be for the use of the treasury of the United States; and all such laws shall be subject to the revision and control of the Congress.

No state shall, without the consent of Congress, lay any duty of tonnage, keep troops, or ships of war in time of peace, enter into any agreement or compact with another state, or with a foreign power, or engage in war, unless actually invaded, or in such imminent danger as will not admit of delay.

Article II EXECUTIVE POWER

Section 1: THE EXECUTIVE POWER shall be vested in a President of the United States of America. He shall hold his office during the term of four years, and, together with the Vice President, chosen for the same term, be elected, as follows:

Each state shall appoint, in such manner as the Legislature thereof may direct, a number of electors, equal to the whole number of Senators and Representatives to which the State may be entitled in the Congress: but no Senator or Representative, or person holding an office of trust or profit under the United States, shall be appointed an elector.

The electors shall meet in their respective states, and vote by ballot for two persons, of whom one at least shall not be an inhabitant of the same state with themselves. And they shall make a list of all the persons voted for, and of the number of votes for each; which list they shall sign and certify, and transmit sealed to the seat of the government of the United States, directed to the President of the Senate. The President of the Senate shall, in the presence of the Senate and House of Representatives, open all the certificates, and the votes shall then be counted. The person having the greatest number of votes shall be the President, if such number be a majority of the whole number of electors appointed; and if there be more than one who have such majority, and have an equal number of votes, then the House of Representatives shall immediately choose by ballot one of them for President; and if no person have a majority, then from the five highest on the list the said House shall in like manner choose the President. But in choosing the President, the votes shall be taken by States, the representation from each state having one vote; A quorum for this purpose shall consist of a member or members from two thirds of the states, and a majority of all the states shall be necessary to a choice. In every case, after the choice of the President, the person having the greatest number of votes of the electors shall be the Vice President. But if there should remain two or more who have equal votes, the Senate shall choose from them by ballot the Vice President.

The Congress may determine the time of choosing the electors, and the day on which they shall give their votes; which day shall be the same throughout the United States.

No person except a natural born citizen, or a citizen of the United States, at the time of the adoption of this Constitution, shall be eligible to the office of President; neither shall any person be eligible to that office who shall not have attained to the age of thirty five years, and been fourteen Years a resident within the United States.

In case of the removal of the President from office, or of his death, resignation, or inability to discharge the powers and duties of the said office, the same shall devolve on the Vice President, and the Congress may by law provide for the case of removal, death, resignation or inability, both of the President and Vice President, declaring what officer shall then act as President, and such officer shall act accordingly, until the disability be removed, or a President shall be elected.

The President shall, at stated times, receive for his services, a compensation, which shall neither be increased nor diminished during the period for which he shall have been elected, and he shall not receive within that period any other emolument from the United States, or any of them.

Before he enter on the execution of his office, he shall take the following oath or affirmation:--"I do solemnly swear (or affirm) that I will faithfully execute the office of President of the United States, and will to the best of my ability, preserve, protect and defend the Constitution of the United States."

Section 2: The President shall be commander in chief of the Army and Navy of the United States, and of the militia of the several states, when called into the actual service of the United States; he may require the opinion, in writing, of the principal officer in each of the executive departments, upon any subject relating to the duties of their respective offices, and he shall have power to grant reprieves and pardons for offenses against the United States, except in cases of impeachment.

He shall have power, by and with the advice and consent of the Senate, to make treaties, provided two thirds of the Senators present concur; and he shall nominate, and by and with the advice and consent of the Senate, shall appoint ambassadors, other public ministers and consuls, judges of the Supreme Court, and all other officers of the United States, whose appointments are not herein otherwise provided for, and which shall be established by law: but the Congress may by law vest the appointment of such inferior officers, as they think proper, in the President alone, in the courts of law, or in the heads of departments.

The President shall have power to fill up all vacancies that may happen during the recess of the Senate, by granting commissions which shall expire at the end of their next session.

Section 3: He shall from time to time give to the Congress information of the state of the union, and recommend to their consideration such measures as he shall judge necessary and expedient; he may, on extraordinary occasions, convene both Houses, or either of them, and in case of disagreement between them, with respect to the time of adjournment, he may adjourn them to such time as he shall think proper; he shall receive ambassadors and other public ministers; he shall take care that the laws be faithfully executed, and shall commission all the officers of the United States.

Section 4: The President, Vice President and all civil officers of the United States, shall be removed from office on impeachment for, and conviction of, treason, bribery, or other high crimes and misdemeanors.

Article III JUDICIAL POWER

Section 1: THE JUDICIAL POWER OF THE UNITED STATES, shall be vested in one Supreme Court, and in such inferior courts as the Congress may from time to time ordain and establish. The judges, both of the supreme and inferior courts, shall hold their offices during good behaviour, and shall, at stated times, receive for their services, a compensation, which shall not be diminished during their continuance in office.

Section 2: The judicial power shall extend to all cases, in law and equity, arising under this Constitution, the laws of the United States, and treaties made, or which shall be made, under their authority;--to all cases affecting ambassadors, other public ministers and consuls;--to all cases of admiralty and maritime jurisdiction;-- to controversies to which the United States shall be a party;--to controversies between two or more states;-- between a state and citizens of another state;-- between citizens of different states;-- between citizens of the same state claiming lands under grants of different states, and between a state, or the citizens thereof, and foreign states, citizens or subjects.

In all cases affecting ambassadors, other public ministers and consuls, and those in which a state shall be party, the Supreme Court shall have original jurisdiction. In all the other cases before mentioned, the Supreme Court shall have appellate jurisdiction, both as to law and fact, with such exceptions, and under such regulations as the Congress shall make. The trial of all crimes, except in cases of impeachment, shall be by jury; and such trial shall be held in the state where the said crimes shall have been committed; but when not committed within any state, the trial shall be at such place or places as the Congress may by law have directed.

Section 3: Treason against the United States, shall consist only in levying war against them, or in adhering to their enemies, giving them aid and comfort. No person shall be convicted of treason unless on the testimony of two witnesses to the same overt act, or on confession in open court.

The Congress shall have power to declare the punishment of treason, but no attainder of treason shall work corruption of blood, or forfeiture except during the life of the person attainted.

Article IV

Section 1: Full faith and credit shall be given in each state to the public acts, records, and judicial proceedings of every other state. And the Congress may by general laws prescribe the manner in which such acts, records, and proceedings shall be proved, and the effect thereof.

Section 2: The citizens of each state shall be entitled to all privileges and immunities of citizens in the several states.

A person charged in any state with treason, felony, or other crime, who shall flee from justice, and be found in another state, shall on demand of the executive authority of the state from which he fled, be delivered up, to be removed to the state having jurisdiction of the crime.

No person held to service or labor in one state, under the laws thereof, escaping into another, shall, in
consequence of any law or regulation therein, be discharged from such service or labor, but shall be delivered up on claim of the party to whom such service or labor may be due.

Section 3: New states may be admitted by the Congress into this union; but no new states shall be formed or erected within the jurisdiction of any other state; nor any state be formed by the junction of two or more states, or parts of states, without the consent of the legislatures of the states concerned as well as of the Congress.

The Congress shall have power to dispose of and make all needful rules and regulations respecting the territory or other property belonging to the United States; and nothing in this Constitution shall be so construed as to prejudice any claims of the United States, or of any particular state.

Section 4: The United States shall guarantee to every state in this union a republican form of government, and shall protect each of them against invasion; and on application of the legislature, or of the executive (when the legislature cannot be convened) against domestic violence.

Article V

The Congress, whenever two thirds of both houses shall deem it necessary, shall propose amendments to this Constitution, or, on the application of the legislatures of two thirds of the several states, shall call a convention for proposing amendments, which, in either case, shall be valid to all intents and purposes, as part of this Constitution, when ratified by the legislatures of three fourths of the several states, or by conventions in three fourths thereof, as the one or the other mode of ratification may be proposed by the Congress; provided that no amendment which may be made prior to the year one thousand eight hundred and eight shall in any manner affect the first and fourth clauses in the ninth section of the first article; and that no state, without its consent, shall be deprived of its equal suffrage in the Senate.

Article VI

All debts contracted and engagements entered into, before the adoption of this Constitution, shall be as valid against the United States under this Constitution, as under the Confederation.

This Constitution, and the laws of the United States which shall be made in pursuance thereof; and all treaties made, or which shall be made, under the authority of the United States, shall be the supreme law of the land; and the judges in every state shall be bound thereby, anything in the Constitution or laws of any State to the contrary notwithstanding.

The Senators and Representatives before mentioned, and the members of the several state legislatures, and all executive and judicial officers, both of the United States and of the several states, shall be bound by oath or affirmation, to support this Constitution; but no religious test shall ever be required as a qualification to any office or public trust under the United States.

Article VII

The ratification of the conventions of nine states, shall be sufficient for the establishment of this Constitution between the states so ratifying the same.

Done in convention by the unanimous consent of the states present the seventeenth day of September in the year of our Lord one thousand seven hundred and eighty seven and of the independence of the United States of America the twelfth. In witness whereof We have hereunto subscribed our Names,

---

G. Washington-President and deputy from Virginia

New Hampshire: John Langdon, Nicholas Gilman

Massachusetts: Nathaniel Gorham, Rufus King

Connecticut: Wm: Saml. Johnson, Roger Sherman

New York: Alexander Hamilton New Jersey: Wil: Livingston, David Brearly, Wm. Paterson, Jona: Dayton

Pennsylvania: B. Franklin, Thomas Mifflin, Robt. Morris, Geo. Clymer, Thos. Fitz Simons, Jared Ingersoll, James Wilson, Gouv Morris

Delaware: Geo: Read, Gunning Bedford jun, John Dickinson, Richard Bassett, Jaco: Broom

Maryland: James McHenry, Dan of St Thos. Jenifer, Danl Carroll

Virginia: John Blair--, James Madison Jr.

North Carolina: Wm. Blount, Richd. Dobbs Spaight, Hu Williamson

South Carolina: J. Rutledge, Charles Cotesworth Pinckney, Charles Pinckney, Pierce Butler

Georgia: William Few, Abr Baldwin Tyranny

OUR FOUNDING FATHERS WROTE TO THIS GENERATION CONCERNING LIBERTY SAYING:

<u>John Adams</u>; *"You will never know how much it has cost my generation to preserve your freedom. I hope you will make a good use of it."*

<u>Benjamin Franklin</u>; *"Those that can give up essential liberty to gain a little temporary safety deserve neither liberty nor safety."*

<u>Samuel Adams</u>; *"If ye love wealth better than liberty, the tranquility of servitude better than the animating contest of freedom, go home from us in peace. We ask not your counsels or your arms. Crouch down and lick the hands which feed you. May your chains set lightly upon you, and may posterity forget that you were our countrymen."*

<u>James Monroe</u>; *"Of the liberty of conscience in matters of religious faith, of speech and of the press; of the trial by jury in civil and criminal cases; of the benefit of the writ of habeas corpus; of the right to keep and bear arms...If these rights are well defined, and secured against encroachment, it is impossible that government should ever degenerate into tyranny."*

<u>George Washington</u>; "*Virtue or morality is a necessary spring of popular government.*"

<u>Benjamin Franklin</u>; "*Only a virtuous people are capable of freedom. As nations become more corrupt and vicious, they have more need of masters.*"

"Laws without morals are in vain."

<u>Benjamin Franklin</u>; "*Sell not virtue to purchase wealth, nor Liberty to purchase power.*"

<u>Thomas Jefferson</u>; "*A nation as a society forms a moral person, and every member of it is personally responsible for his society.*"

<u>Thomas Jefferson</u>; "*No government can continue good but under the control of the people; and . . . . their minds are to be informed by education what is right and what wrong; to be encouraged in habits of virtue and to be deterred from those of vice . . . . These are the inculcations necessary to render the people a sure basis for the structure and order of government.*"

<u>James Madison</u>; "*To suppose that any form of government will secure liberty or happiness without any virtue in the people is a chimerical idea.*"

<u>Patrick Henry</u>; "*Virtue, morality, and religion this is the armor, my friend, and this alone that renders us invincible. These are the tactics we should study. If we lose these, we are conquered, fallen indeed so long as our manners and principles remain sound, there is no danger.*"

<u>Patrick Henry</u>; "*Bad men cannot make good citizens. It is when a people forget God that tyrants forge their chains. A vitiated state of morals, a corrupted public conscience, is incompatible with freedom. No free government, or the blessings of liberty, can be preserved to any people but by a firm adherence to justice, moderation, temperance, frugality, and virtue; and by a frequent recurrence to fundamental principles.*"

<u>John Adams</u>; "*The only foundation of a free Constitution is pure Virtue, and if this cannot be inspired into our People, in a great Measure, than they have it now. They may change their Rulers, and the forms of Government, but they will not obtain a lasting Liberty.*"

<u>John Adams</u>; "*Our Constitution was made only for a moral and religious people. It is wholly inadequate to the government of any other.*"

<u>John Adams</u>; "*Liberty can no more exist without virtue and independence than the body can live and move without a soul.*"

<u>John Adams</u>; "*Public virtue cannot exist in a nation without private, and public virtue is the only foundation of republics.*"

John Adams; "*It is religion and morality alone which can establish the principles upon which freedom can securely stand. The only foundation of a free constitution is pure virtue.*"

<u>John Adams</u>; "*The laws of man may bind him in chains or may put him to death, but they never can make him wise, virtuous, or happy.*"

<u>John Adams</u>; "*Statesmen, my dear Sir, may plan and speculate for liberty, but it is religion and morality alone, which can establish the principles upon which freedom can securely stand. The only foundation of a free Constitution is pure virtue, and if this cannot be inspired into our People in a greater Measure than they have it now, they may change their rulers and the forms of government, but they will not obtain a lasting liberty.*"

John Adams; "*Honor is truly sacred, but holds a lower rank in the scale of moral excellence than virtue. Indeed the former is part of the latter, and consequently has not equal pretensions to support a frame of government productive of human happiness.*"

Fisher Ames; "*Our liberty depends on our education, our laws, and habits it is founded on morals and religion, whose authority reigns in the heart, and on the influence all these produce on public opinion before that opinion governs rulers.*"

Richard Henry Lee; "*It is certainly true that a popular government cannot flourish without virtue in the people.*"

Thomas Paine; "*Whenever we are planning for posterity, we ought to remember that virtue is not hereditary.*"

Samuel Adams; "*Neither the wisest constitution nor the wisest laws will secure the liberty and happiness of a people whose manners are universally corrupt. He therefore is the truest friend of the liberty of his country who tries most to promote its virtue, and who, so far as his power and influence extend, will not suffer a man to be chosen onto any office of power and trust who is not a wise and virtuous man.*"

Samuel Adams; "*The diminution of public virtue is usually attended with that of public happiness, and the public liberty will not long survive the total extinction of morals.*"

"If the public safety be provided, liberty and propriety secured, justice administered, virtue encouraged, vice suppressed, and the true interest of the nation advanced, the ends of government are accomplished . . ."
Algernon Sidney

Benjamin Rush; "*Liberty without virtue would be no blessing to us.*"

Benjamin Rush; "*Without virtue there can be no liberty.*"

Benjamin Rush; "*The only foundation for... a republic is to be laid in Religion. Without this there can be no virtue, and without virtue there can be no liberty, and liberty is the object and life of all republican governments.*"

Andrew Jackson; "*No free government can stand without virtue in the people, and a lofty spirit of patriotism.*"

Daniel Webster; "*Our ancestors established their system of government on morality and religious sentiment. Moral habits, they believed, cannot safely be on any other foundation than religious principle, nor any government be secure which is not supported by moral habits.*"

Daniel Webster; "*If we and our posterity reject religious instruction and authority, violate the rules of eternal justice, trifle with the injunctions of morality, and recklessly destroy the political constitution which holds us together, no man can tell how sudden a catastrophe may overwhelm us, that shall bury all our glory in profound obscurity.*"

<u>Frederick Douglas</u>; "*The life of the nation is secure only while the nation is honest, truthful and virtuous.*"

<u>Northwest Ordinance of 1787</u>; "*Religion, morality and knowledge, being necessary to good government and the happiness of mankind, schools and the means of education shall be forever encouraged.*"

<u>Proverbs 14:34</u>; "*Righteousness exalteth a nation.*"

<u>Edmund Burke</u>; "*Men are qualified for civil liberty in exact proportion to their disposition to put moral chains upon their appetites; in proportion as their love of justice is above their rapacity; in proportion as their soundness and sobriety of understanding is above their vanity and presumption; in proportion as they are more disposed to listen to the counsel of the wise and good, in preference to the flattery of knaves. Society cannot exist unless a controlling power upon will and appetite be placed somewhere, and the less of it there is within, the more there must be without. It is ordained in the eternal constitution of things, that men of intemperate minds cannot be free. Their passions forge their fetters.*"

<u>Daniel Webster</u>; "*If we and our posterity reject religious instruction and authority, violate the rules of eternal justice, trifle with the injunctions of morality, and recklessly destroy the political constitution which holds us together, no man can tell how sudden a catastrophe may overwhelm*

us, that shall bury all our glory in profound obscurity."

Ronald Reagan; "*A state is nothing more than a reflection of its citizens; the more decent the citizens, the more decent the state.*"

Thomas Jefferson; "*When virtue is banished, ambition invades the minds of those who are disposed to receive it and avarice possesses the whole community.*"

Thomas Jefferson; "*Dependence begets subservience and venality, suffocates the germ of virtue, and prepares fit tools for the designs of ambition.*"

Thomas Jefferson; "*Liberty . . . is the great parent of science and of virtue; and . . . a nation will be great in both always in proportion as it is free.*"

Thomas Jefferson; "*The order of nature [is] that individual happiness shall be inseparable from the practice of virtue.*"

Thomas Jefferson; "*Without virtue, happiness cannot be.*"

Alexander Hamilton; "*The institution of delegated power implies that there is a portion of virtue and honor among mankind which may be a reasonable foundation of confidence.*"

Printed in Great Britain
by Amazon